Nēnē

Nēnē

MARION COSTE

ILLUSTRATED BY CISSY GRAY

A KOLOWALU BOOK
University of Hawaii Press
Honolulu

For the children of Hawai'i and the world, we are pleased to help make possible this valuable resource. We hope that knowledge will transform to motivation to protect Hawai'i's endangered species.

On behalf of our employees and their families who live and work in Hawai'i, PRI is proud to support Nēnē.

BHP PETROLEUM/PACIFIC RESOURCES

Library of Congress Cataloging-in-Publication Data
Coste, Marion, 1938–
Nēnē / Marion Coste ; illustrated by Cissy Gray.
p. cm.
"A Kolowalu Book."
Summary: Describes the physical characteristics and habits
of the nene, or Hawaiian goose, and the problems that have
threatened its survival.
ISBN 0-8248-1389-8
1. Nene—Hawaii—Juvenile literature.   [1. Nene.   2. Geese—
Hawaii.   3. Rare animals.]   I. Gray, Cissy, ill.   II. Title.
QL696.A52C67   1993
598.4'1—dc20   92-36543   CIP   AC

Printed in Singapore

www.uhpress.hawaii.edu

Dedication

To the children of Hawai'i, who hold the future of the islands in their hands and hearts

Acknowledgments

Thanks to Ron Bachman, Paul Banko, Howard Hoshide, Bob Leinau, Nelson Santos, Carol Terry, and Ron Walker for their help, and to the late Wayne Gagné for his inspiration.

The sun rises over the volcano. It is a yellow autumn sun, warming the land after the cool night. In the grass under the pūkiawe bush, the nēnē stirs. She has been tending her three eggs for a full month.

She listens, head tilted to one side. Small sounds are coming from the eggs. Perhaps today is the day they will open. Perhaps today she will see her babies at last.

Nearby, the male nēnē
ruffles his feathers and stretches
his neck to greet the day. He has
stayed close by the nest watching for
danger ever since the eggs were laid. But
the days have been quiet: no mongoose has
crept through the thick grass to steal the eggs;
no wild pig has come rooting through the bushes,
scattering the nest.

The male nēnē rises up on his long black legs
and flaps his wings. He would fight to save his nest.

The female steps off the nest. She turns to look closely at the eggs. She can see small cracks in two of them. The babies are beginning to peck their way through the hard white shell. She watches the chicks struggle to come out. The male looks over from his rocky perch.

It is tiring work to get through the shell. The first baby chick finally breaks out and lies panting on the twigs and soft down that make the floor of the nest. His feathers, wet from the egg, stick to his small body. His heart pounds.

Soon the other two eggs are broken open and two more goslings lie resting in the nest. The sun and warm breeze soothe them and dry their feathers. By the time the sun is high in the afternoon sky, the three goslings are dry and fluffy, their soft gray down more like fur than feathers.

Mother and father nēnē are hungry. They wander off slowly to find some sweet berries and tender grass shoots. The goslings run behind and between them. Although less than a day old, the chicks are able to scurry along on their sturdy black legs.

They cannot fly yet. They must wait until strong flight feathers grow on their wings. This is a dangerous time for the goslings: they cannot take to the air to escape from animals or people who might hurt them. The parents stay with them, protecting them and leading them to food.

The nēnē family must watch for cats, rats, and mongooses that like to catch and eat the young goslings, and hunters who shoot or trap the adults. They stay close to the grass and bushes so they can hide if danger threatens. Their gray-brown feathers blend into the colors of the plants and rock that are their home.

On the barren lava field, the small goslings can hide in cracks.

As darkness falls, the nēnē family finds a spot to rest. The goslings nestle near the female, and she spreads her feathers to cover her babies from the cool night dampness.

The male nēnē settles down not far away, resting on the dusty ground, head tucked under one wing.

Soon all black eyes are closed, and moonrise finds the family asleep.

The nēnē stay in their rocky home through the cool and rainy winter months, searching for food during the day and resting together at night.

One day while the nēnē are busy eating, a mongoose creeps up unseen and catches one of the goslings with his needle-sharp teeth.

Another gosling is carried off by a cat on a dark night. The parents and one last gosling stay close together.

After a few weeks, the gosling loses his fuzzy down and his wings begin to show shiny flight feathers. Soon he will fly.

Now begins the parents' time of danger. They are molting: old feathers fall out and new ones grow in. For two months, the adult nēnē cannot fly. The family travels back to the safety of the nesting area.

By summer, the parents' new feathers are full and strong. It's time to fly. The three nēnē fly higher up the volcano slope to find the tasty grasses and berries of the new season. Other nēnē families join them.

There are not as many families now as in years gone by, when nēnē flocked from the lands near the sea to the high mountain uplands. Do these birds know about those ancient days, when nēnē flew freely around the islands? The grass grew thick on land without houses or roads, and the woods held no mongooses or wild pigs.

Long ages ago, nēnē could roam wherever the sweet grass grew. Their only enemies were hawks and owls. No predators stalked the wild land searching for food. The nēnē made nests farther and farther away from water. Their legs grew long and sturdy; the swimmer's webbing between their toes began to disappear. They learned to live with rain, wind, and the hot summer sun.

Life changed for the nēnē when humans came to the islands. Early Hawaiians discovered the nēnē were good to eat; the feathers useful for capes and kāhili. After generations without enemies, the nēnē were easy to catch. They did not sense danger and did not fly away.

The forests were cut and burned and the grasslands cleared to build villages and farms and roads.

The nēnē lost their home. The people who came to live on the islands brought new animals: rats, pigs, and later cats and mongooses that liked to eat the eggs and tender young goslings of the ground-nesting nēnē. Cows, horses, and goats trampled the bushes and nesting areas. The nēnē did not understand these dangers and did not know how to protect themselves. They began to disappear.

Nesting grounds were gone, feeding grounds were gone, and the nēnē were almost gone, too. Fewer than fifty nēnē remained alive in the wild. The nēnē had become an endangered species, animals who might disappear from the Earth.

At last, laws were passed to protect these native Hawaiian birds. Some wild areas where nēnē lived were fenced to keep out animals and people. Young nēnē, raised in pens, were released into the fenced areas. Scientists and rangers watched as the new wild nēnē began to find food, build nests, and raise families.

The days grow shorter, and the nēnē leave the uplands and return to the nesting areas lower on the side of the volcano. Family group by family group, they rise into the sky for the flight down the mountain.

They return to the same nesting place they left in the summer. The restless winds and roaming animals have scattered the remains of last year's nest.

Last year's gosling is a gander now, and he must leave his family. He will live with other young geese for the next year or two, then find a mate and start his own family.

The female nēnē begins to scoop a shallow hole out of the grass and leaves under the protecting pūkiawe bush. Soon she will lay new eggs and prepare for the long time of brooding.

The male stands in the grass nearby. He looks around, bright black eyes searching for signs of danger. He is the protector.

Shadows lengthen. The sun begins its slow descent behind the volcano. The female nēnē climbs into the nest, tucking her slender neck behind one wing.

The male ruffles his feathers and settles down to rest. The sky blazes briefly with pink and gold, then darkens.

The sun sets on the nēnē.

Information about the Nēnē

Scientific name: *Nesochen sandvicensis*
Common name: Hawaiian goose
Hawaii state bird

Description

The nēnē is a medium-sized goose with the typical long neck, long legs, and fat body of a goose. It can grow as tall as twenty inches and weigh up to five pounds. The head, back of the neck, beak, and feet are black. The wing and back feathers are gray-brown with white bars. The breast is light brown. The tail is black with a white underside. The nēnē has yellowish cheek and neck feathers with deep rows of dark feathers running from cheek to breast. A black band circles the base of the neck. The feet have some webbing between the toes. The male and female look alike, but the male is slightly larger. Scientists have identified two calls: a soft, murmuring "nay-nay," and a loud cry used when territory is threatened.

Habitat

Most wild nēnē live on high mountain slopes and lava flows. They build their nests in places where plants give them some shelter. Before humans came to Hawai'i, the nēnē ranged from sea level to the grassy upper mountain slopes. Scientists think the nēnē once lived on most of the major Hawaiian islands, but today they are found only on Hawai'i, Maui, and Kaua'i. They still have no fear of humans and have been known to nest on the inviting grass of golf courses.

Food

A nēnē eats grasses, green leafy plants, berries, and seeds. Among its favorites are crabgrass, 'ohelo, sow thistle, gosmore, and *pūkiawe*.

Nesting and Breeding

Unlike most geese, the nēnē nests in the winter, from November to March. The female scoops a shallow nest in the ground and lays two to five cream-colored eggs. She pulls soft down feathers from her breast to tuck around the eggs. Only the female sits on the nest, leaving it for short periods to find food. The male stands guard nearby. The incubation period is twenty-eight to thirty days. Nēnē mate for life and are two or three years old when they build their first nest and lay eggs.

Care of the Young

The goslings are gray, with black beaks and dark gray legs and feet. They have at least four different calls, which many scientists think are "pleasure," "greeting," "sleepy," and "distress" signals. The adult nēnē guard the goslings carefully, keeping the young ones between them when they move in exposed areas. The goslings do not fly for about eleven to fourteen weeks after hatching. When the adults complete their molt in summer, the family group flies together to feeding grounds. The goslings stay with the adults for a full year.

Defense

When threatened, a nēnē will bend its neck, lower its body, quiver its neck feathers, and hiss or make loud calls. Captive nēnē have been known to bite. The coloring of the feathers gives the nēnē some camouflage. The female may try to fool watchers about the location of her nest: she sneaks away from it with her head and body low to the ground, then stands upright and shows herself in a different place.

Adaptations

Scientists think the nēnē descended from Canada geese that landed on Hawai'i long before humans arrived. As they survived on the isolated islands for generation after generation, the geese gradually changed, becoming a new species. Today's nēnē, unlike its water-loving ancestor, is a land bird. The nēnē's legs are longer than those of the Canada goose, the pads on the bottom of its feet are much thicker, its toenails are longer and stronger, and the webbing between its toes is only about half as long. The wingspan is slightly shorter than the wingspan of other geese, and the nēnē builds its nest during the shorter days of the winter months, while other geese nest during the spring and summer. The nēnē is able to swim, but can get along without water in its habitat. It gets enough liquid in its diet from the young grass shoots and berries it eats.

Population

The nēnē is the rarest goose in the world. Scientists estimate that before Captain Cook's arrival in 1778 there were about twenty-five thousand wild nēnē in Hawai'i. By 1952, the population had dropped to fewer than thirty individuals. In 1991, approximately five hundred nēnē lived in the wild.

Problems

The Hawaiians sometimes hunted the nēnē for meat and feathers, which they used to make capes and *kāhili*. As they cleared away the forests and grasslands for villages and farms, the habitat of the nēnē began to disappear. Other peoples arrived and used more of the land for homes, roads, more farms and towns.

Some of the animals they brought with them ate the plants the nēnē fed on, and others preyed on the nēnē eggs, young birds, and nesting females. Hunters did not understand the life cycle of the nēnē and set a hunting season in the winter, when the nēnē, nesting and taking care of their young, could not escape.

The nēnē retreated up the mountain slopes until they lived only in the higher elevations, where food was sparse. Their numbers dwindled.

Today, problems still plague the wild nēnē. Sometimes hunters shoot the nēnē, even though such killing is against the law. The native Hawaiian plants the nēnē eat are getting more and more scarce. Cats, pigs, dogs, and mongooses attack the geese, especially the tender goslings, and goats, sheep, pigs, and humans destroy the nēnē's habitat.

Recovery

In 1949, two pairs of nēnē were loaned to the Hawaii Board of Agriculture and Forestry by Herbert Shipman, a rancher on the island of Hawai'i. These four geese were the beginning of a breeding program designed to raise nēnē in captivity and release them into the wild. The nēnē were placed in pens at Pōhakuloa on Hawai'i, where they nested and reared families. When the healthy young nēnē were old enough, they were allowed to fly free. Fences around the release areas helped keep out animals that might attack the nēnē or damage the nesting sites.

At the same time, another pair of nēnē from Mr. Shipman's flock was sent to the Wildlife Trust in Slimbridge, England. In 1962, some of the nēnē raised in England were brought to Maui, carried in Boy Scouts' backpacks up the slope of Haleakalā, and released in the crater of the dormant volcano.

Soon the captive nēnē flocks grew larger, and more geese were released into the wild. The United States government gave money to the Fish and Wildlife Service to keep the release program going. The nesting area on Hawai'i was declared a sanctuary.

The goal of the Nene Restoration Program was to have two thousand wild nēnē living on the island of Hawai'i and two hundred fifty on Maui. Since the beginning of the program in 1949, two thousand nēnē have been released, and today's population of wild greese is about five hundred.

Even though the program has increased the number of wild nēnē, scientists do not think these birds can live successfully without human help. Their problems seem to be overwhelming, and until scientists can find ways to make the habitats better and keep predators away, the nēnē will continue to walk on the edge of extinction.

Captive nēnē are kept at several zoos and animal parks around the world, and a large flock still lives at Slimbridge.

Protection

The nēnē was listed as an endangered species by the United States government on March 11, 1967. The Endangered Species Act was passed in 1973, making it unlawful to import, export, harass, harm, pursue, hunt, shoot, wound, kill, trap, capture, collect, or even have in your possession any endangered species unless you have a federal permit. The nēnē is also protected by the federal Migratory Bird Treaty Act and Hawaii state law.

In Hawaii, the agencies responsible for the protection of the nēnē are the Hawaii Division of Forestry and Wildlife of the Department of Land and Natural Resources, the U.S. Fish and Wildlife Service, and the National Park Service.

Glossary

adaptation - change in an animal's body structure or behavior that enables it to survive in a certain place

barren - having little or no plant life

brooding - sitting on and hatching or protecting eggs

camouflage - the color (and sometimes behavior) of an animal that enables it to blend into its surroundings

crabgrass - a grassy weed that spreads quickly because it has stems that will take root. Some people think it looks like a crab. Nēnē eat the leaves and seeds.

dormant - no longer active; quiet, still

down - soft, fine feathers

endangered species - animals or plants that may become extinct

extinct - no longer exists on Earth

gander - a male goose

gosling - a baby goose

gosmore - a tall, thin-stemmed weed that looks like a dandelion. Also called the long-rooted catsear. Nēnē eat gosmore seeds, leaves, stems, and flowers.

habitat - the area in which an animal lives and can find all it needs to survive

Haleakalā - a dormant volcano on the island of Maui. The name means "home of the Sun."

incubation - the sitting on or hatching of eggs

kāhili - long poles with feathers fastened to the top, symbolic of Hawaiian royalty

life cycle - the changes an animal or plant goes through from birth to death

molting - shedding or losing body covering, such as fur or feathers

mongoose - a small, meat-eating, furry mammal that looks like a weasel

native - belonging to or found in a certain location, such as Hawai'i, without having been brought by humans

'ohelo - a bush with small, flat leaves and bright red berries that grows at elevations of three thousand feet or higher. Nēnē eat the berries.

predators - animals that hunt and eat other animals

pūkiawe - a thick-leafed bush with light green leaves and clusters of  small red and white fruit. Nēnē eat the fruit, and scientists think the stones in the fruit help the birds digest their food.

sanctuary - a safe place for animals, where they should not be bothered by people

sow thistle - a weed with yellow flowers and spiny leaves. Also called *pualele*.

wingspan - the measure of a bird's wings from tip to tip

About the Author

Marion Coste graduated from Connecticut College and has been an elementary school teacher and an educator/administrator at Mystic Marinelife Aquarium, Bishop Museum, Honolulu Academy of Arts, and the Hawaii Children's Museum. She has worked as a trainer/consultant for The Kamehameha Schools and is a lecturer in the College of Education, University of Hawaii. She was awarded a 1991 nonfiction grant from the Society of Children's Book Writers.

About the Illustrator

Cissy Gray, award-winning artist and portrait painter, resides in Seattle. She was educated at Connecticut College and the Seattle Art Institute and has taught marketing design. She is a former partner in two art galleries in Honolulu and a member of many art guilds across the United States. She has illustrated children's books—among them *To Find the Way*—as well as magazines.